They Are Real

© 2013 by Robert Conners All rights reserved.
Published 2013

Published by VIP Ink Publishing

Cover Design and Editing By Whyte Lady Designs L.L.C.

www.vipinkpublishing.com

ISBN 13: 978-0-9847382-9-8
ISBN: 0-9847382-9-8

Printed in the USA.

No part of this book may be reproduced, stored in a retrieval system, or transmitted, in any form or by any means, electronic or mechanical, including photocopying and recording without prior written permission from the publisher.

They Are Real

By: Robert Conners

Table of Contents

Introduction.......................... i

Chapter 1: The Reality and Pervasiveness of the UFO Phenomenon..................... 1

Chapter 2:The Bible and UFOs.......... 8

Chapter 3: UFOs and the Place of Christian Apologetics......................... 12

Chapter 4: Some Characteristics of the UFO Phenomenon.......................... 17

Chapter 5: The Extraterrestrial Hypothesis 21

Chapter 6: The God-Astronaut Theory... 26

Chapter 7: The Ingenious Substitute Religion............................... 29

Chapter 8: "Manipulating" Matter? — The Capabilities of Angels................ 42

Chapter 9: Pertinent Passages for Examining the UFO Phenomenon.................... 47

Chapter 10: A Theological Framework for the Space-Age............................. 58

Chapter 11: A Christian Response to a Modern Trend................................. 67

Chapter 12: UFOs - Does Anybody Care? The Need for a Cutting-Edge Apologetic.... 74

Introduction

UFOs[1]…our culture is fascinated with them. From television programs and cinema movies to documentaries on so called alien abductions, we are bombarded with the idea of life from other worlds. Indeed many are convinced of the truthfulness of these claims.

If alien beings really are visiting us, their presence is most definitely one of the major news stories of all time. But what portion of the reports is accurate? And when genuine, how are we to interpret this information? Have space alien's invaded earth, or are there other potential explanations?

While different groups within society have taken their shot at interpreting UFOs, few Christians have entered the fray. This book is designed to briefly touch upon some facets of the UFO phenomenon from a biblical perspective. While offering no exhaustive answers, we hope to remain consistent with both the Bible's teachings and current knowledge of UFOs.

---

[1]The term UFO is used here in a broad sense to refer to the entire UFO phenomenon. This includes "sightings" of various kinds, as well as the ideas often mentioned in connection with them. Many automatically equate UFOs with extraterrestrial intelligences; but for some interesting comments on the psychic aspects of the phenomenon, see Jacques Vallee, *Dimensions: A Casebook of Alien Contact* (New York: Ballantine Books, 1988), pp. 159-160

For many Christians, the subject of UFOs seems far-fetched and irrelevant. After all, isn't this the subject of tabloid news and crackpots? But against the idea that UFOs can be easily dismissed are the reports of sound researchers, the many reliable eyewitnesses, & the countless individuals who have been influenced by what might be termed alien religion.

Of course, there is a side to this topic that is ludicrous, or at least humorous. Beneath the surface, however, there looms a huge UFO movement. This UFO sub-culture and those influenced by it have, for the most part, accepted what must be considered one of the most captivating and illusive belief systems ever promulgated.

The Christian Church has a responsibility to subject various ideologies to biblical scrutiny. That is, believers should be able to place current trends, movements, and world views under the lens of Scripture. For the most part, apologists[2] have done ample research in a number of areas. But our apologetic should include not only traditional elements (i.e. cults), but more

---

[2] From the Greek apologia, meaning "defense." Apologetics is "that branch of Christian theology which has as its aim the reasoned advocacy of the Christian faith." Millard Erickson, *Concise Dictionary of Christian Theology* (Grand Rapids: Baker Book House, 1986), p. 14. John M. Frame defines apologetics as "the discipline that teaches Christians how to give a reason for their hope." *Apologetics to the Glory of God* (Phillipsburg, NJ: Presbyterian & Reformed Publishing Company, 1994), p. 1. At some level, therefore, we are all Christian apologists.

bizarre factors such as UFOs. To that end, this publication is designed to be a thought-provoking resource. The time has come for Christians to offer a biblically informed and intelligent perspective on this far reaching phenomenon.

In other words, I will present a broad framework for analyzing UFOs, especially from the standpoint of biblical revelation. What follows are general observations, guidelines and a supporting structure for the Christian who wishes to investigate this baffling phenomenon.

Chapter 1: The Reality and Pervasiveness of the UFO Phenomenon

UFOs have greatly influenced the thoughts and perception of modern man, though the subject is treated in numerous ways. Running the gamut from the ridiculous portrayals expressed in tabloid circles to the serious, even religious, perspective of those caught up in the movement; its pervasiveness is undeniable.

Furthermore, it is not easy to discount the entire movement on the basis of its lunatic fringe. Many of its proponents are too sound in mind to simply ignore, and those who have had first-hand contact with "aliens" (whatever they are) are sometimes of such reputable character that pretending the phenomenon doesn't exist is no longer a valid option.

The Reality of UFOs

It is difficult to prove to some that the concept of UFOs is worth investigating because so many ludicrous stories have been promulgated. Broaching the subject is most often met with a less than serious reaction. Admittedly, even serious students of ufology need to occasionally scratch their heads and wonder whether any of this can possibly be real. No doubt, many readers who study this subject do so blushingly. After all, science-fiction cannot be coming true...or can it?

But against the idea that this phenomenon is to be treated as a childish fascination is the clear cut evidence that something is actually occurring. Craziness aside, and some of this truly fits within that category, this subject has been tackled by a good number of sane individuals.

Allen Hynek, for instance, was one of the premier scientists involved in the government's Operation Blue Book, an investigation of UFOs. After eliminating the obviously false or mistaken reports of UFOs, Hynek concluded that there is a legitimate category of genuine unidentified phenomena. His research is scientifically based, honest, and not given to absurdities. If even a small percentage of the alleged UFO sightings, abductions, and messages are true, this is a phenomenon of major proportions.

More recently, Jacques Vallee, a French computer scientist and physicist, has shown himself to be a top-notch investigator. He has researched the subject of UFOs for many years, and a perusal of his works surely precludes the notion that he is an extremist. On the contrary, his work exudes integrity as he engages this subject in a sound and stimulating manner.

To this list could be added the names of many others. While their interpretations of the phenomenon may differ, they all seem to agree that "something" really is going on.

Then there are many accounts of what appear to be very stable individuals describing amazing occurrences. Some have seen, or even videotaped, phenomena which defy natural explanation; others have had experiences so traumatic that their perception of reality has been forever altered. The entire worldview of a growing number of people has shifted because of encounters with UFOs.

On top of what has already been mentioned, there are countless people who while not having a UFO encounter themselves, have nonetheless bought into the idea that some of what they've heard or read about is real. In fact there are a number of groups and organizations which specialize in the study, analyses, and promotion the UFO phenomenon[3]. Some have even produced rather scholarly works on various aspects of this subject. At any rate, a wealth of legitimate data gives credence to the factualness of this mysterious phenomenon.

The Pervasiveness of the UFO Phenomenon
Not only is there legitimacy to the notion of a real UFO phenomenon, but this phenomenon is pervasive[4]. The concept of

---

[3]These include the Center for UFO Studies (CUFOS), the Mutual UFO Network (MUFON), and a host of others.
[4]The whole concept of aliens has become something of a trend in society. In our day, you can find an alien or a UFO associated

UFOs has so affected modern thought that people hardly blink when some alien theory is proposed by one of its adherents.

Look at your TV guide; visit the local movie theater. It won't be long before you begin to see a UFO agenda emerging. The details will vary, of course, but there is unquestionably some sort of alien mind-set being foisted (innocently or not) upon our generation.

Examine the New Age section of your local bookstore and you will find a multiplicity of books detailing, in one form or another, the belief in UFOs; often these are written from a religious or spiritual perspective.

Listing all of the popular UFO literature would obviously take up too much space, and the list is constantly growing. But in order to show the pervasiveness of this phenomenon, here is a sampling of the much larger body of UFO-related literature[5].

➢ *Abduction: Human Encounters with Aliens* by John Mack - Scribners – 1994
➢ *Aliens - The Final Answer: A UFO*

---

with everything from candy, T shirts, and automobile commercials to more serious-minded pursuits such as the many web sites on the World Wide Web. Of course, much of this is harmless, and many groups use the UFO genre merely as a means of drawing attention to their product or area of interest. Whatever the implications, however, it would be difficult to miss the prevalence of UFOs in the modern world.

[5]One listing on the Internet included over 400 titles on the subject of UFOs!

Cosmology for the 21st Century by David Barclay - Blanford Press – 1996

➤ *Anatomy of a Phenomenon: Unidentified Objects in Space -- A Scientific Appraisal* By Jacques Vallee - Ballantine Books – 1974

➤ *Beyond The Four Dimensions: Reconciling Physics, Parapsychology, and UFOs* by Karl Brunstein - Walker – 1979

➤ *Close Encounters of the Fourth Kind: Alien Abduction, UFOs and the Conference at M.I.T* By C.D.B Bryan - Penguin USA – 1996

➤ *Extraterrestrials in Biblical Prophecy* by G. Schellhorn - Horus House – 1990

➤ *Extraterrestrials: Life in Outer Space* by Amanda Davis - Rosen Pub Group – 1997

➤ *Genesis Revisited* By Zecharia Sitchin - Avon – 1990

➤ *God Drives a Flying Saucer* by R. L. Dione - Exposition Press – 1969

➤ *Guardians of the Universe?* By Ronald Story - St. Martin's Press – 1980

➤ *Into The Fringe* by Karla Turner - Berkeley Books – 1992

➤ *Jesus Christ: Heir to the Astronauts* by G. Steinhauser - Abelard - Schuman – 1974

➤ *Lost Realms* by Zecharia Sitchin - Bear & Co – 1990

➤ *Masquerade of Angels* by Karla Turner - Kelt Works – 1994

➤ *Messengers of Deception: UFO Contacts And Cults* By Jacques Vallee - Berkeley Books – 1979

➤ *Missing Time: A Documented Study of UFO*

Abductions by Budd Hopkins - Richard Marek – 1981
➢ *Paranormal Phenomena: Opposing Viewpoints* by Paul A. Winters – 1997
➢ *Preparing For Contact: A Metamorphosis of Consciousness* by Lyssa Royal - Royal Priest Research – 1993
➢ *Secret Life: Firsthand Accounts of UFO Abductions* by David Jacobs - Simon & Schuster – 1992
➢ *The Bible and Flying Saucers* by Barry Downing - J.B. Lippincott – 1968
➢ *The Eyes of the Sphinx: The Newest Evidence of Extraterrestrial Contact in Ancient Egypt* by Erich Von Daniken – Berkley Pub – 1996
➢ *The God Hypothesis: Extraterrestrial Life and Its Implications for Science and Religion* By Joe Lewels - Wild Flower Press – 1997
➢ *The Gods of Eden* by William Bramley - Avon – 1990
➢ *The Great Airship Mystery: A Urfa of the 1890's* By Daniel Cohen - Dood Mead – 1981
➢ *The Gulf Breeze Sightings* by Ed Walters & Frances – Avon – 1990
➢ *The Omega Project, Nde, UFO Encounters and the Mind At Large* By Kenneth Ring - William Morrow – 1992

➢ *The Secret School: Preparation for Contact* by Whitley Strieber - Harper Collins – 1997
➢ *Transformation: The Breakthrough* by Whitley Strieber - William Morrow – 1988

- *UFO's And the Alien Presence: Six Viewpoints* by Michael Lindemann - The 2020 Group - 1991
- *UFO's, Space Brothers & The Aquarian Age* By Joshua Shapiro - Des Plaines, V J Enterprises - 1987
- *UFO's: Operation Trojan Horse* By John Keel - 1970

Examples could easily be multiplied. The point is that the UFO phenomenon has infiltrated our culture, affecting the ideas of massive numbers of people.

Furthermore, the claim being made by some UFO authors (and by the so-called aliens whom they allegedly interpret and/or represent) is that this phenomenon so intertwines mankind's origin and destiny that its full disclosure might lead to a societal paradigm shift. That is, the discovery of the true nature of UFOs may open up a reality of such magnitude that the world will never be the same again. Much of the popular literature on the subject surely lends itself to this interpretation, for there is an unmistakable religious element to alien theories.

Chapter 2: The Bible and UFOs

Though the earth is not geocentrically[6] located it is important to recognize that the human race is central to God's redemptive activity. Scripture tells us that the heavens have been created to display God's glory to humanity (Ps 19:1-6)[7]. Earth is the place where God spoke in Old and New Testament times (Heb 1:1-2). The Son of God became an inhabitant of this world. He lived, died, and came back to life here. Earth is the location of His eventual return and reign (Matt 24:30-31).

Obviously, then, God is supremely concerned with the race of Adam. God's creative and saving purposes are fulfilled on this third planet from the sun. Of course this does not eliminate the possibility of life on other worlds. All I can say is that other races, if they exist, are not mentioned in the Bible[8].

This is not surprising, though, for the Bible is given to members of this fallen

---

[6]Located at the center of the solar system/galaxy/universe

[7]Admittedly, the wonder of God's creation is evident to all creatures, wherever their particular location. Contextually, however, the people in view in Psalm 19 are members of the human race.

[8]It might be argued that a number of non-human creatures are mentioned in Scripture (e.g. angels, principalities, powers, elders), and that we aren't given clear indication as to their characteristics. Perhaps, then, some of these "entities" might be construed as being extraterrestrial in nature. Yet such a position is at least difficult to support from many of the relevant texts.

race. Thus the Bible is a complete and sufficient message from God. But nowhere does it claim to answer every matter of human interest or speculation.

Since the Bible doesn't speak to the subject of life on other planets, it is theoretically possible that extraterrestrial life exists[9]. What we need to understand, therefore, is that the discovery of non-human intelligence does not, in the least, threaten the biblical portrait. Should an alien intervention take place, Christianity will survive.

As fascinating, and even astounding, as such a close encounter might be, the Christian's relationship with God wouldn't change.

Though a measure of speculation is inevitable when dealing with such an unusual topic, perhaps a few words should be said about our theoretical space

---

[9] Some, including Christians, have stated that this universe is simply too large for God not to have created life elsewhere. But those who make such assertions are viewing the universe as rather empty, apart from the existence of beings to occupy it. Though God's creatures (men, angels, aliens?) play a fundamental role in God's plan, there is no real need to assume that a certain number of these beings must exist somewhere in the vastness of outer space. After all, the Bible says the heavens primary purpose is to declare God's glory. Also, those who feel that huge portions of our universe would be "wasted space" apart from other life-forms, must still deal with the fact that even if there are other alien cultures, these exist at extremely remote distances from one another. Thus there will always be gigantic sections of space which, by the nature of the case, remain uninhabited by intelligent life as we know it.

visitors. If they exist, as popularly believed, they are the product of God's creative hand. Life on other planets would not prove atheistic evolution to be true. On the contrary, it would give evidence that God has been at work in other segments of the cosmos. Since all life-forms are necessarily a part of God's handiwork, it follows that they would be subject to Him.

If UFOs make contact, they do so under God's sovereign permission. Any interaction with our culture can only occur within God's providence and for His own purposes. Also it can be assumed that the Scriptures would, at least in the broadest sense, apply to these creatures. Though the specifics of the plan of redemption seem intended for believers within the human race, the basic tenets of Scripture would be applicable to extraterrestrials.

For instance, alien creatures would not have the authority to intervene in our world in an immoral way. They would not be able to, say, murder people without moral consequence. Perhaps, as depicted in many a science-fiction movie, they would have the ability to conquer the human race. But they would never have the moral right to do so. Such behavior would have to be deemed ungodly.

This also opens up the issue of possible satanic influence. It appears that Satan, given divine permission, would be able to manipulate foreign creatures as he does members of our world. He is, after all, "the prince and power of the air" (Eph 2:2). The world is his domain (1 John 5:19). This makes us wonder whether or not these theoretical space beings are members of a fallen race, which would in turn lead us to deeper levels of speculation beyond the scope of this book [10] . If not greatly edifying, it is at least interesting food for thought.

While there are a number of problems with the ET hypothesis, believers needn't be philosophically opposed to such an idea. The Christian's world view would not be greatly affected by proof of their existence (Romans 8:35-39). If beings from outer space arrive on our planet (or already have arrived) and fill the skies with their alien hardware, the Christian's basic perspective remains intact.

---

[10] For some stimulating thinking on exo-theology (the theological implications of extraterrestrial life) see Ted Peters, "Exo-Theology: Speculations on Extraterrestrial Life," in *The God's Have Landed: New Religions from Outer Space*, ed. James R. Lewis (New York: State University of the New York Press, 1995), pp. 187-206.

Chapter 3: UFOs and the Place of Christian Apologetics

The Church has often been guilty of gross ignorance when it comes to contemporary challenges. Christians are notorious for responding to queries long after the fact. A philosophy takes hold of a segment of society, and believers are slow to give an answer. Some idea seeps into the conscience of modern man, and it goes un-commented upon by the Christian community [11]. This is obviously true concerning our response to the UFO phenomenon. Though the concept of UFOs has touched countless millions of people, it is rarely mentioned by modern apologists[12]. With notable exceptions, the subject is either covered in an overly simplistic fashion or ignored outright. Perhaps, then, it is time for Christians to comment from a biblical foundation as to

---

[11] Unfortunately, when it comes to new challenges that confront the Church, not many operate on the "cutting edge." Few, it seems, have their lives planted in both the biblical world and contemporary culture. Those who lack biblical perspective possess little basis for making a sound apologetic. On the other hand, those who don't regularly look at the world (through Christian lenses) are apt to have an antiquated understanding of the real "happenings" in today's world. While apologists continue to comment (and rightly so) on such areas as the cults, not enough have given adequate time to analyzing current moral/philosophical/spiritual trends (e.g. the influence of religious pluralism, neo-paganism, UFOs).

[12] *"Nine percent of the U.S. population claims to have seen what they believe to be a UFO, and half the people who think of UFOs as a reality believe they come from outer space. Our culture is shot through with space consciousness. One would expect, therefore, that theological leaders would want to respond to the rise in space consciousness by providing some intellectual guidance. Yet, surprisingly, relatively little is being done."* Ted Peters, "Exo-Theology" in The Gods Have Landed, p. 193.

what this puzzling and quite influential phenomenon entails. Long overdue is the need for modern defenders of the faith to give a Christ-honoring perspective on this mysterious topic.

Apologetics, from the Greek apologia, is that aspect of Christian theology and ministry in which the relevance and intelligibility of the gospel are highlighted. The Christian apologist seeks to define, defend, and show forth the attractiveness of Christian revelation. While apologetics can take on various forms, it should be seen, minimally, as what Peter termed "always being ready to make a defense to everyone who asks you to give an account for the hope that is in you" (1 Pet 3:15)[13].

Among other factors, the Christian's starting point is the Lordship of Jesus Christ. Peter tells us, "sanctify (set apart) Christ as Lord in your hearts." The unbeliever may have limited success in his investigative efforts. But those who approach life from the perspective of

---

[13] See especially John M. Frame, *Apologetics to the Glory of God* (Phillipsburg, NJ: Presbyterian and Reformed Publishing Company, 1994). Also see his *The Doctrine of the Knowledge of God* (Phillipsburg, NJ: Presbyterian and Reformed Publishing Company, 1987), pp. 87-88, 347-368. There he defines apologetics as "the application of Scripture to unbelief" (p. 87). McGrath says apologetics is "the attempt to create an intellectual climate favorable to Christian faith" or "a concern to enhance the public plausibility of the gospel." Alister McGrath, *Evangelicalism and the Future of Christianity* (Downers Grove, IL: Intervarsity Press, 1995), p. 102. Apologetics, then, is multifaceted. It involves displaying the beauty and coherence of biblical Christianity.

biblical faith have a distinct advantage, for they alone possess an infallible framework.

"Far from stopping questions, belief in God can liberate inquiry."[14] Skeptics no doubt can, and should, learn from their observations (Rom 1:19-20). A truly Christian apologetic, however, should not start with the skeptic's presuppositions. Instead the believer investigates in the subject of UFOs, not from some supposedly neutral standpoint, but from the perspective of those already convinced that God has unambiguously spoken, both in general (Romans 1:19-20) and special revelation (Hebrews 1:1-2).

Our apologia, then, must ultimately lead to a defense and explanation of the Christian faith in the context of current societal trends. One such example is that generated belief in UFOs. But before arriving at a truly Christian outlook on this phenomenon, it is imperative to understand the matter of hermeneutics.

Hermeneutics involves the proper use of those principles and tools which lead to an accurate understanding of the biblical text[15]. The goal is to determine what the

---

[14]David Wilkinson, *Alone in the Universe?* (Crow borough: Monarch Publications), p. 107.

[15] On the subject of hermeneutics see Grant R. Osborne, *The Hermeneutical Spiral* (Downers Grove, IL: Intervarsity Press, 1991). Also very helpful is D. A. Carson's introductory essay,

Bible says. In order for this to occur in a truly Christian way, however, the centrality and authority of God's Word must be maintained. The Scriptures are no ordinary documents, subject to the whims of the interpreter. Rather, they are God's message to mankind (Ps 19:7-11; 2 Tim 3:16)[16]. What this means is that UFOs must be studied from a biblical perspective, not the other way around[17].

The Christian apologist views the world, first of all, through the lens of scripture truth. This might be portrayed as follows:

➤ The right (Christian) approach: Through the lens of THE BIBLE ---> analysis of UFOs.
➤ The wrong approach: Through the lens of UFOLOGY ---> analysis of the Bible.

The second approach is given to fanciful and forced interpretations of the biblical record. The first approach, on the other hand, is only interested in accurately perceiving what God has spoken through His chosen authors. This is not to say that the

---

"Approaching the Bible" in *New Bible Commentary: 21st Century Edition*, ed. D. A. Carson, R. T. France, J. A. Motyer, G. J. Wenham (Downers Grove, IL: InterVarsity Press), pp. 1-19.

[16]For an explanation and defense of Christian epistemology and biblical authority see *The Doctrine of the Knowledge of God*, pp. 123-164; J. I. Packer, *God Has Spoken: Revelation and the Bible* (Grand Rapids: Baker Books, 1979, 1993); and Clark H. Pinnock, *Biblical Revelation* (Chicago, IL: Moody Press, 1971).

[17] See John A. Saliba, "Religious Dimensions of UFO Phenomena" in *The God's Have Landed*, pp. 33-34.

Christian should reject any valid insights from ufology and the like. If there is information which might enhance our overall knowledge it should be considered. But the text itself always takes priority, not a desire to force an agenda into it. Because God has spoken, His Word is the only proper starting point for constructing an apologetic.

Chapter 4: Some Characteristics of the UFO Phenomenon

One needs merely watch a few movies, listen to some of the recent claims, or read the popular literature to realize that there is a dark side to the UFO phenomenon. This can take a number of different forms, some of which are briefly outlined here.

First, there is clearly a New Age flavor to many of the UFO accounts. A brief perusal of the literature makes this very evident. These unidentified craft/beings are believed by many to be harbingers of a new era, a time of peace and tranquility. The Age of Aquarius, as some would term it, is about to dawn. Those from within this camp view the entire UFO phenomenon as a religious movement. We are ready to take a cosmic leap to a new and higher spiritual plain.

Also many are saying these alien visitors are here to protect us from ourselves, shielding humanity from nuclear obliteration and various calamities. So, for instance, they desire to facilitate the protection (worship?) of the environment. Supposedly, they want mankind to live in harmony with one another and all of nature.

Strange as it may seem, however, the extraterrestrials sound much like contemporary politicians. But it is highly unlikely that advanced creatures from some distant planet would take up an agenda that coincides with the modern (and imbalanced) philosophies of the politically correct. At the least, it sounds suspicious[18].

Next there is the abduction experience. If we are to believe the claims, many people have been forcibly taken as prisoners, poked, prodded, and put through a series of sexual experiments that would amount to space rape. Whatever else this reveals, we are surely dealing with thoughts and events which are the antithesis of biblical teaching.

Then there is the matter that certain UFO encounters resemble occult activity. Levitation, walk-ins (in which higher beings "walk into" or possess humans) and other occurrences are claimed by some. In days gone by, these would have been viewed by the Christian community as demonic in nature. If and when they occur within the UFO movement, they should probably still be placed within that category.

What's more, UFO appearances have also been associated with religious groups and practices which evangelical Christians have traditionally labeled misleading,

---

[18] Indeed, it sounds like the same forces which influence so many within our post-modern culture have surfaced in segments of the UFO community. Could this mean that the "principalities and powers" responsible for errors in society at large are active in the UFO movement?

false, or heretical. For instance, the alleged apparitions of Mary at Fatima (and elsewhere) are rightly rejected for portraying her in ways clearly out of line with Christian theology. Likewise, Mormon history and beliefs are heterodox. Yet both of these share some common-ground with aspects of the UFO phenomenon[19].

But perhaps the most alarming messages from "alien" visitors are those which directly contradict the Bible's teachings. Sometimes the Christian gospel is subtly denied, while on other occasions the attack is more direct. There are those who even postulate that Jesus was merely an advanced human or an alien.

At any rate, the consistent message is one in which Jesus Christ is demeaned and His role minimized. Clearly this can only be labeled anti-Christian, and part of the Satanic system which seeks to thwart God's plan (1 John 2:21-24; 4:1-3; 5:10). Whether these ideas originate from organized human groups, the imaginations of the UFO fanatic, alien civilizations, or spiritual forces; they can often be classified as unbiblical. For the Christian, this is cause for concern.

---

[19] See *Dimensions*, pp.173-195. In this section, Vallee, who is not a Christian, shows some of the parallels between UFOs and certain religious apparitions. What is striking is the fact that the religious events which Vallee highlights are basically those which fall outside the parameters of evangelical Christianity. In other words, Vallee unwittingly weds UFOs to bogus or unbiblical groups and concepts.

This review is obviously not enough to render infallible answers as to the specific identity of UFOs. It should cause honest investigators to pause, however, before too hastily assuming their benevolence. You can, after all, determine a tree by its fruit (Matthew 7:15-20). And the fruit produced by at least certain portions of this movement is of a poison variety. Now this shouldn't be construed as a wholesale rejection of all UFO research. Nor is the "New Age" tendency necessarily part-and-parcel of every aspect of ufology. It's just that the phenomenon, while intriguing, warrants serious theological discernment. Therefore it necessary to proceed carefully and honestly, desiring only right-mindedness and biblical consistency.

Chapter 5: The Extraterrestrial Hypothesis

The current belief among most popular ufologists is that UFOs are of extraterrestrial origin. They are usually viewed as somebody else's "nuts and bolts" craft, occupied by advanced beings from somewhere in distant space (or another dimension).

Typical of the ideas that swirl around the belief in UFOs are the following:

➢ The world's governments are well-aware of alien beings but have been involved in a massive cover-up/conspiracy;
➢ UFOs are known to have crashed, and the bodies of deceased aliens have been examined by government scientists;
➢ Abductions are real physical "kidnappings" which occur (possibly) for the purpose of ensuring the survival of the alien's civilization; this is accomplished by means of the fertilization of women who now carry space babies;
➢ UFOs are here to assist mankind, like big space brothers should. They are concerned for humanity's survival, and want us to pursue global peace;

…and so the story goes.

As mentioned earlier, this scenario is so

consistently repeated that few appear willing to offer other explanations. And when alternate theories are put forth, most simply ignore them in order not to rock the UFO "boat" (ship?). Still, some investigators feel less than enthused about the ET hypothesis.

First of all, one has to wonder about the reliability of many of the UFO reports. Some UFO reports are highly suspicious, and the trustworthiness of the informants often suspect[20]. Someone appears to be expending great energy trying to convince the public to accept the ET theory. Maybe this is because it actually represents the truth, …or maybe not.

Questions also emerge when trying to make sense of the alleged UFO sightings and their typical explanations. Highly unlikely is the theory that advanced beings need us to promulgate their race. And it is puzzling, to say the least, that "aliens" desire to make their presence known (e.g., crop circles, sightings and abductions) while simultaneously appearing reluctant to disclose their full identity. Surely an

---

[20]We should note that a great number of those claiming to have been abducted discover and remember their experience through regressive hypnosis. Concerning this use of hypnosis by UFO researchers, Vallee says, "It is not simply misguided, it is irresponsible, unscientific and profoundly unethical." *Dimensions*, p. 274. This is not to suggest that all UFO memories are simply "made up." It does make one question, however, whether the stories we hear are all legitimate. Likewise, one has to ask whether extraterrestrial intelligences are the real cause of these abduction experiences, if and when they actually occur.

advanced race, one which has managed to travel to earth from far-away places, would be able to remain completely undetected. But they're not hiding themselves.

On the other hand, clear-cut, unambiguous evidence is hard to come by. The usual explanation: They are hiding from us until we are ready to receive them. Are we to believe, then, that these incredibly secretive beings hide their very identity at the highest level, while simultaneously allowing us to observe them via movie cameras and other personal encounters? Such a scenario, that UFOs are both meticulous professionals of secrecy and bumbling alien idiots who seem to leave traces of themselves everywhere, is difficult to accept [21]. All of this seems rather inconsistent with the idea of aliens from outer space.

This is not to mention the massive distances these alleged aliens would need to traverse in order to arrive on this planet. Of course, there is always someone who will argue for a "worm hole" [22] theory, and

---

[21]A tantalizing explanation for this mixture of hidden-ness (i.e., "they" won't plainly appear) and disclosure (i.e., apparently "they" want us to see them from a distance) is that the UFO occupants are involved in some sort of deception. That is, they carry out their agenda, convincing many of their existence and significance. At the same time, they won't allow us to get too close, lest we discover their true identity.

[22]A "wormhole" is a theoretical concept involving interstellar tunnels which are considered by some to be links between black holes. Supposedly, a space traveler might be able to enter a black hole in one part of the universe and exit at an entirely different

perhaps such an idea will prove to be valid. One wonders, though, why not a few ufologists are willing to abandon current knowledge on the basis of pure speculation. Perhaps the UFO agenda has so consumed some enthusiasts that it has reached religious proportions. Indeed, it apparently has.

Current knowledge does not preclude the possibility of an extraterrestrial explanation for UFOs; the theory shouldn't be rejected out of hand. But there is reason to remain skeptical, and this skepticism is shared by others. One such individual is Jacques Vallee. He was a close associate of Dr. J. Allen Hynek, whom many consider the father of UFO research. Vallee later served as the real-life model for a character in Steven Spielberg's film Close Encounters of the Third Kind. His knowledge of physics and computer science, along with his extensive research of this phenomenon, make him one of the premier experts in the field.

Concerning the extraterrestrial theory, Vallee argues, "Exciting as an extraterrestrial visitation to earth would be…in the current state of our knowledge, the UFO phenomena are not consistent with the common interpretation of this hypothesis." [23] He continues, "The inescapable conclusion is that the people

location. Thus the wormhole might be thought of as a type of cosmic shortcut. See *Alone in the Universe?* pp. 80-84.

[23] Jacques Vallee, *Revelations* (New York: Ballantine Books, 1991), pp. 277-278.

who claim so vocally to expose the cover-up may be the ones who constitute the cover-up itself. Somebody is going to a lot of trouble to convince us of the reality of extraterrestrials, to the exclusion of other, possibly more important hypotheses about UFOs."[24] Whatever else might be said about UFOs, it is reasonable to test the validity of the ET theory. Maybe they are from other worlds. That would be amazing enough. But if this explanation proves inadequate, UFOs might represent an even deeper mystery.

---

[24]*Revelations*, p. 185. Also, *Five Arguments Against the Extraterrestrial Origin of Unidentified Flying Objects*, pp. 261-279.

Chapter 6: The God-Astronaut Theory

Erich von Däniken popularized the idea that the appearances of God in the Bible were actually UFO encounters[25]. Primitive man, so the story goes, was not able to grapple with the great technology of extraterrestrial visitors, and therefore mistook these aliens for divine beings. Thus the miracles and wonders of the Bible quite likely took place, and needn't be denied. They must simply be reinterpreted in light of current knowledge and the presumed technology of our space brothers.

The God-astronaut theory has been promoted by others as well. More recently, Zecharia Sitchin has taken up a line of argument in which the God of Scripture is replaced by a god of immense technology[26]. This idea is also fostered by numerous television shows and movies. Those who approach the Bible with this presupposition find it quite easy to interpret a cloud as a spaceship, or a resurrection as a feat of medical genius.

---

[25]Erich von Däniken's books include *Chariots of the Gods?*; *God's from Outer Space* and *Gold of the Gods*. Among von Däniken's theories is that the destruction of Sodom and Gomorrah recorded in Genesis 19:1-28 was actually an atomic explosion. Many such claims permeate his works. These conjectures are taken up and refuted specifically by Clifford Wilson in his *Crash Go the Chariots* (New York: Lancer Books, 1972), and *The Chariots Still Crash* (Old Tappan, NJ: Spire Books, 1975). Also see Ronald Story, *The Space-Gods Revealed* (New York: Barnes & Noble Books, 1977).
[26]Sitchin's works include a series entitled *The Earth Chronicles* (5 books in all), and *Genesis Revisited* (New York: Avon Books, 1990). Sitchin bases much of this conjecture on his interpretation of information acquired from the ancient Sumerian civilization (in today's southern Iraq).

Proponents of this theory are committed to finding UFOs, convinced as they are that biblical religion is a record of extraterrestrial creatures, not an all-powerful deity.

That the God of the Bible might have actually been some sort of alien life form is an increasingly popular thought. Besides the numerous books on the subject, there have been of late a variety of science fiction programs making similar claims. One recent television show (presumably fictional) tells of an Episcopal pastor who is forced to face up to the reality that UFOs may invalidate all of his previously held religious beliefs.

The underlying assumption is that traditional Christian interpretations will have to be abandoned because all of life's mysteries will be explainable in terms of advanced extraterrestrial visitors.

This highlights what many people believe, that UFOs are the missing link in the quest to know more about man's origin and place in the universe. After all, if UFOs are capable of such amazing feats, traditional religion might be seen as meaningless.

Many, many people are being exposed to this type of pseudo-scientific mentality. Discerning Christians know such influence affects the way people think about matters of ultimate importance. Therefore,

believers must learn to counter the
arguments for outer space religion.

Chapter 7: The Ingenious Substitute Religion

Throughout history there have been many attempts to deny or twist the Christian message. During the early years of the Church, various heterodox teachings arose concerning God, Christ, and the locus of divine revelation. Fortunately the Church (in God's grace and providence) responded by grounding its theological formulations in the apostolic testimony derived from Scripture.

In recent times, the attacks have been of a more skeptical nature. Surely, the biblical writings aren't to be accepted at face value. Modern man cannot be expected to believe the Scriptures record literal truth. Along these lines, many now-famous arguments have been devised by which we can "better understand" what the Bible records.

Jesus' resurrection, for instance, has been interpreted in many ways. Some prefer to believe that the resurrection is nothing more than a fable added to the Christian tradition long after the fact. Others have conjured up elaborate explanations in order to deny the historical evidence. Of course, one major problem with these theories is that they tend to ignore all or part of the Bible's story line. As might be expected, then, many Christian apologists have displayed the inconsistencies and contradictions inherent in these liberal theologies[27].

UFO religion, however, represents an entirely different brand of attack on historical Christianity. Proponents of the God-astronaut hypothesis don't necessarily reject the basic historicity of the Old and New Testaments. In that sense, they represent a less skeptical brand of interpretation. In fact, they often attempt to assimilate biblical events into their theories. Rather than attacking its contents and denying its basis in history, they accept much (if not all) of what the Bible records. At the same time, though, there is a strong denial that God is all the Scriptural writers claim He is. Proponents of the God-astronaut theory do this by plugging the UFO phenomenon and extraterrestrial hypothesis into the biblical text.

Their reasoning is something as follows: *The people of Bible times were, for the most part, sincere and reliable individuals. Therefore what they record is probably, in the main, an accurate reflection of what they thought they had witnessed. Their limitation, though, was that they didn't have the technological know-how of modern man, and so they erred in their*

---

[27]E.g., J. Gresham Machen, *Christianity and Liberalism* (1923; Grand Rapids: Wm. B. Eerdmans Publishing Company, 1990), J. I. Packer, *Fundamentalism and the Word of God* (1958; Grand Rapids: Wm B. Eerdmans Publishing Company, 1988).

*interpretations   of   what   actually
transpired.*

In   other   words,   the   biblical
authors/characters had enough sense to know
they had observed "something," but recorded
their observations in light of their own
antiquated presuppositions. They weren't
able to identify a space ship, so they
labeled it a cloud. Miracles were merely the
misidentified medical practices of an
advanced alien culture.

The God-Astronaut hypothesis, and the
religion it spawns, represents a very
clever attempt to deal with the biblical
data while simultaneously denying its very
basis. On the surface such an argument looks
plausible. But closer scrutiny reveals some
glaring weakness in the theory of religion
from the stars.

➤ Those who want to find UFOs everywhere in
   the Bible are usually quite sloppy when
   it comes to interpreting the biblical
   texts.

   o Because their ultimate allegiance is
     elsewhere, UFO enthusiasts are not
     usually   careful   students   of
     Scripture. For many, the alien agenda
     has so consumed them that they are
     unable   to   honestly   interpret   a
     passage. Thus they tend to construct
     flawed interpretations of historical
     events,   and   so   misrepresent   the

original author's meaning.

The only sure way to accurately interpret the Bible (or any literature) is by letting it speak for itself. In other words, the only valid guide to interpretation is exegesis. This means interpreters must not force their assumptions into the text. The goal, rather, must be to determine what the biblical authors intended to convey by the words they penned. Fanciful interpretations may capture the imagination, but they misrepresent the Bible's message.

One common example where ufologists mishandle a biblical text is the now famous case of Ezekiel's encounter with God (Ezekiel 1:4-28). Those who wish to find flying saucers in the ancient writings look for support in such places as this. Ezekiel's "wheels," for instance, are thought to be UFOs. A closer look at the passage, however, shows how fallacious this interpretation is. The so-called UFOs are actually part of a vision which Ezekiel receives from God (v. 1). A vision, of course, is not an actual physical manifestation, as would be the case, presumably, in a UFO encounter. In fact, Ezekiel's companions apparently remained unaware of what had transpired. Therefore, what might sound like evidence to be marshaled in favor of the UFO phenomenon is actually nothing of the sort.

"By picking some elements out of context, reading into the particular verses things you want to see, and by frankly manipulating the words of the text to suggest something that it is not, and then it is possible to claim this was an alien spacecraft. This all shows the danger of inaccurate research.[28]"

➢ If UFOs are responsible for the contents of the biblical record we are left with the same problem which C.S. Lewis defined years ago, the tri-lemma?

o A number of years ago, C. S. Lewis spoke of what has often been referred to as the trilema of Christ. Many in his day (and in ours as well) tried to manufacture a Jesus devoid of the supernatural, a man with admirable qualities but only a man. Such has often been the case. Whatever the specifics, men seek to reconstruct Jesus in a manner which fits their preconceived notions. Not surprisingly, He is nearly always portrayed as something less than divine.

---

[28]Wilkinson, *Alone in the Universe?* p. 104.

But Jesus hasn't left us with such an ambiguous portrait of Himself. No man could make the claims He made and still be considered a good and honest individual. This is where the trilema comes into play:

- Either Jesus was not telling the truth when He claimed to be the Son of God—in which case He was a colossal liar,
- or He sincerely believed Himself to be that which He obviously was not—thus inviting the label of delusional,
- or He was who He claimed to be—the eternal Word made flesh, the Lord from heaven (John 1:14).

These are the only reasonable options: Lord, liar, or lunatic. Lewis's famous words are worth quoting: *"I am trying here to prevent anyone saying the really foolish thing that people often say about Him: 'I'm ready to accept Jesus as a great moral teacher; but I don't accept His claim to be God.' That is the one thing we must not say. A man who was merely a man and said the sort of things that Jesus said would not be a great moral teacher. He would either be a lunatic—on a level with the man who says he is a poached egg.—or else he would be the Devil of Hell. You must make your choice. Either this man was, and is, the Son of God: or else a madman or something worse. You can shut Him up for a fool, you can spit at Him and kill Him as a demon; or you can fall at His feet and call Him Lord and God. But let us not come up with any patronizing nonsense about His being a great human teacher. He has not left that open to us. He did not intend to."*[29]

Obviously, since Jesus is neither deceiver nor crazy man, He must be the divine Messiah. This same truth applies when considering the claims that Jesus was actually an alien, and not the Son of God. Here is a theory which promotes the belief that Jesus was an honest individual, a teacher of righteousness. But what of his stupendous claims, claims of equality with God and the like (Mark 2:5; John 5:23; 8:58)? To deny He uttered such words contradicts the wealth of evidence to the contrary [30]. Acknowledging that Jesus made such claims but deceived his hearers in doing so, puts us back in "Lewis territory."

---

[29]C.S. Lewis, *Mere Christianity* (1943; New York: Simon & Schuster Publishers, 1996), p. 56.

[30] For a defense of the orthodox portrait of Jesus, see Gregory A. Boyd, *Cynic, Sage or Son of God?* (Wheaton, IL: Victor Books, 1995), Gary R. Habermas, *The Historical Jesus: Ancient Evidence for the Life of Christ* (Joplin, MO: College Press Publishing Company, 1996), and Luke Timothy Johnson, *The Real Jesus: The Misguided Quest for the Historical Jesus and the Truth of the Traditional Gospels* (New York: Harper Collins Publishers, 1996).

How could a good man, a wonderful model of all that is right, be so outlandishly misguided or deceptive when it comes to his very identity? Good men tend not to promote their own worship. Decent people aren't apt to freely accept adoration. Men of marvelous character don't make claims of deity. The Jesus was an alien concept just doesn't make sense. If He was an alien (or was manipulated by them—the situation remains the same either way), Christendom must face up to what must be the most devastating act of deception in the history of mankind.

All fair-minded individuals must ask why a supposedly advanced race, in its attempts to assist humanity, would so mislead us. Why would they build us up only to dash all of our hopes? Again, the theory is neither logically nor psychologically plausible[31].

➢ The people of Bible times are not to be classified as ignorant and uninformed. Had they truly encountered alien craft or some such thing, they would have been able to convey that fact adequately.

---

[31]"The 'Jesus was an astronaut' theory may sound initially attractive, but as you look at the accounts of Jesus, you have to give this alien more and more powers and schemes, when it is truer to the observations to adopt a different explanation. He was God as a human being." *Alone in the Universe?* p. 112.

o Many assume that the people of Bible times were backward and ill equipped to accurately describe their experiences. Therefore technological marvels would appear to them as miracles. But this goes against the available evidence. Though ancient peoples didn't posses advanced scientific knowledge, they did have enough common sense to know the difference between, say, a saucer-shaped object and a cloud. If the biblical writers had truly encountered the aliens described by many ufologists, they would have been able to give reasonably accurate, albeit pre-scientific, descriptions of their experiences[32]. Yet there is little that resembles a full-fledged, modern UFO sighting.

There will always be those who look for, and expect to find, a demon or UFO around every corner. But an evenhanded approach looks for a surer basis for belief, for more than mere conjecture. Of course UFOs may not be extraterrestrial visitors. Instead, they may be better explained as part

---

[32]Far from naive, the early Christians were not even prone to accept a miracle as significant as Jesus' resurrection. When the women at the tomb reported the resurrection, we are told "these words appeared to them as nonsense, and they would not believe them" (Luke 24:11). In other words, the apostles were not predisposed to such events; they had to be convinced!

of a spiritual control system. If so, the mechanisms which under girds the UFO phenomenon may well have played a role, possibly a sinister role, in the unfolding of biblical events.

➤ The Bible and the God of the Bible have changed far too many lives to be relegated to the category of alien history. Furthermore, the internal consistency and inherent authority of Scripture argue for a divine rather than an extraterrestrial or merely human explanation of its existence.

o There is more to apologetics than defending the faith. Christians also have the responsibility of going on the offensive. That being, it is important to lay out the Bible's story line in such a way that its inherent beauty and consistencies are manifest to all who are willing to see.

Biblical Christianity has a remarkable record in that it has been the impetus to positive change in the lives of countless millions throughout history. Individuals, families, even nations, have been forever transformed by the truths of Scripture. The Bible makes claims and promises which have been validated in the lives of different people from many backgrounds in every age. Surely this argues for a divine rather than a high-tech explanation of its origin. Only God can change a human heart; the Bible has been the divine instrument to that end (e.g., Psalm 19:7-11; 119:1, 9, 89, 97, and 114).

The Bible's contents are also a marvelous thing to behold. While we shouldn't minimize the doctrinal disputes which have arisen throughout Church history, it is none-the-less true that the Bible displays an inner coherence. Its teachings make sense, they fit together. The countless volumes on theology are evidence that the Bible is no ordinary book. This, in turn, supports a divine rather than an extraterrestrial explanation for its existence.

The idea of life from outer space has not gone unchallenged. Before closing this section, therefore, it might be helpful to list some of the authors who debunk the God-Astronaut thesis. These include the following:

➢ Alnor, William *UFOs & The New Age: Extraterrestrial Messages and the Truth of Scripture* Grand Rapids: Baker Book House, 1992
➢ Boa, Ken and Proctor, William *The Return of the Star of Bethlehem* Grand Rapids: Zondervan Publishing House, 1980
➢ Lewis, James R, ed. *The God's Have*

Landed: New Religions from Outer Space
New York: State University of the New
York Press, 1995
➢ Rose, Fr. Seraphim *Orthodoxy and the
Religion of the Future*. Platina, CA: St.
Herman of Alaska Brotherhood, 1975
➢ Story, Ronald *The Space-Gods Revealed*
New York: Barnes & Noble Books, 1977
➢ Wilkinson, David *Alone in the Universe?*
Crow borough: Monarch Publications, 1997
➢ Wilson, Clifford *Crash Go the Chariots*
New York: Lancer Books, 1972
➢ Wilson, Clifford *The Chariots Still
Crash* Old Tappan, NJ: Spire Books, 1975
➢ Wimbish, David *Something's Going On Out
There* Old Tappan, NJ: Fleming H. Revell
Company Publishers, 1990

As many of these authors argue, the
substitute religion proposed by certain
ufologists is an inaccurate reflection of
the biblical record. Though there are some
similarities between UFOs and ancient
events, these are usually superficial and
the result of an overly-active imagination.
Furthermore, the fact that the phenomenon
approximates but does not duplicate
historical realities may indicate
something quite sinister. Whatever UFOs
are, the ideas which are sometimes
associated with them look like forgeries.
This means that far from being the key to
unlocking Scripture, the UFO phenomenon
looks more like a clever counterfeit of true
religion.

This doesn't furnish us with complete answers as to the identity and nature of these alien forces. It does, however, show us something of the deceptive nature of the "gods" from outer space.

Chapter 8: "Manipulating" Matter? — The Capabilities of Angels

There have been a number of Christian writers who have labeled the UFO movement Satanic. Unfortunately, though, few display a willingness to look seriously at both the biblical data and the UFO phenomenon itself. To only superficially investigate one or the other is to run the danger of misrepresenting the facts on either side.

Many Christians have only a shallow understanding of the claims and profound evidence presented for UFOs. Because of this, they are prone either to dismiss the movement out-of-hand, or to give shallow (though perhaps accurate) definitions of what UFOs really are. Rarely has anyone put any effort into unfolding the meaning of texts which may prove helpful in an investigation such as this.

Therefore, few have sought to formulate what might be termed a truly biblical perspective on this phenomenon. While UFOs are of secondary importance (at best) to the Christian believer, it would certainly help if those who choose to enter the field in the first place would do so with more intellectual vigor, imagination, biblical literacy, and theological acumen.

While a degree in theology isn't a necessary prerequisite to sound study, investigation within this field must become better informed and more scripturally sound. To that end, it must be asked what biblical category most closely parallels the modern UFO phenomenon. The most plausible answer would seem to be that of angels. While seeking to avoid overly dogmatic assertions, it is reasonable to wonder if a portion of genuine UFO activity falls within this category. This idea can be traced out further.

First, it should be noted that the angelic encounters of the Bible leave the impression that these supernatural creatures are capable of great feats. Genesis 6:2-4, for instance, describes a scene in which "the sons of God" mate with human women. Though commentators debate their identity, some believe angelic beings are in view. If true, this is a scene in which spiritual entities mate with humans. Apparently, angels are capable of taking on physical form and characteristics. How this occurs, of course, is beyond us[33].

---

[33]We should stress here that there is no consensus as to the identity of these "sons of God." In his commentary on 2 Peter, after discussing some of the options of a related passage, Moo cautiously states that "properly nuanced, we need not think it impossible that Genesis 6:1-4 refers to fallen angels who had sexual relations with women." Douglas J. Moo, *2 Peter and Jude* (NIV Application; Grand Rapids: Bondservant Publishing House, 1996), p. 112. See also David Atkinson, *The Message of Genesis 1-11* (BST; Downers Grove, IL: InterVarsity Press, 1990), p. 130. For an evenhanded appraisal which favors the angelic interpretation, see Sydney H.T. Page, *Powers of Evil: A Biblical*

Next, there is Genesis 18:1. Here three "men" appear to Abraham and his wife. The context clearly tells us that one of these "men" is the Lord Himself, while the other two are angels (19:1). All three of these beings take on a physical form, even consuming food (v. 5). Again, spiritual beings manifest themselves in tangible ways.

Then in 2 Kings 6:17 Elisha prays for divine intervention. Suddenly, an invisible army of horses and chariots is revealed to Elisha's servant. Angelic creatures show themselves in the physical realm.

Moving to the New Testament, there are further examples. The "young man" at Jesus tomb (Mark 16:5) is a prime case in which an angel (cf. Matthew 28:2, 5) takes the form of a man. Luke 3:20-21 may represent a similar happening, only here it involves the Holy Spirit Himself. In this scene, the Spirit seems to take on some type of visible form, that of a dove.

These represent only a sampling of what we are trying to show, namely, that non-physical beings have the ability to appear in physical form. Perhaps, they are given temporary "bodies" in order to accomplish their various tasks. Maybe

Study of Satan & Demons (Grand Rapids: Baker Books, 1995), pp. 43-54, 230-237.

spirit beings (or some of them) have the gift of materialization. Though the mechanism involved is impossible to decipher, undeniable is the fact that spirit beings are able to assume a tangible existence.

Given the above perspective, it is easy to see the parallel between the UFO phenomenon and some accounts of angels. Angelic beings can manipulate matter and so project themselves in rather unusual ways. Sometimes they appear as "young men." On other occasions they consume food. At times they show themselves as warriors riding horses and chariots[34].

In other words, UFOs could be some sort of manifestation in which angels project images in a manner compatible with our time frame. Admittedly, such a concept is difficult to fathom. But the unusual behavior of certain UFOs and their occupants, the New Age characteristics inherent in much of the movement, and the unbiblical messages attributed to them, should cause us to consider this as a possible explanation for some part of the phenomenon. UFOs might be explainable within the biblical category of angels.

---

[34] It is worth noting that the vision referred to here (2 Kings 6:17) describes angelic creatures manifesting themselves in ways that conformed to that particular culture. Similarly, and perhaps not by coincidence, modern UFOs are consistent with the expectations of those who live in our high-tech society.

While many within modern society reject the Christian concept of angels, this doesn't hinder these amazing creatures from finding new ways to express themselves. As Keith Thompson hauntingly states: "We may have long ago cast aside our angelic hierarchies, but the demonic has not forgotten where we live, and means to enter through the least secure door…"[35] Perhaps many have been "entertaining" (fallen?) angels with knowing it" (Hebrews 13:2).

---

[35] Keith Thompson, Angels and Aliens (New York: Ballantine Books, 1991), pp. 232-233.

Chapter 9: Pertinent Passages for Examining the UFO Phenomenon

Many claims are being made by UFO believers about the contents of the Bible. As mentioned earlier, these often involve a superficial reading of a number of texts. Usually this amounts to making the Bible conform to the beliefs of the reader. Not only is this improper, it's also dangerous. Of course it is surely right to go to the Scriptures, seeking the wisdom which God has committed to these inspired writings. Thus it is good and proper to investigate UFOs from a biblical perspective. But does the Bible speak to this phenomenon?

First of all, it is improbable that UFOs, in the modern sense, are to be found throughout the biblical record. It may be that some biblical events parallel the modern phenomenon. Perhaps, God even uses UFOs as a mechanism of some sort to carry out His various dealings [36]. Still, Scripture is not a guide to aerial activity and the like.

Having said this, the Bible's applications

---

[36]"To argue that God's heavenly messengers need UFOs to achieve His purposes is to limit God's powers, and His thoughts, to those of men. Much of the modern writing about UFOs and the Bible tends to think of God as little more than a glorified astronaut. The Bible shows Him as omnipresent, omnipotent, and omniscient, and His heavenly servants are not limited by earth's laws of physics. The physical principles by which UFOs operate might well be utilized for the purposes of God, but the Bible certainly does not confine Almighty God to a heavenly 'super-car.'" Clifford Wilson, *The Alien Agenda* (1974; New York: Penguin Books, 1988), pp. 208-209.

to these mysterious happenings shouldn't be minimized. While an analysis of alien space craft is not to be found, certain aspects of the phenomenon are answerable via divine revelation. In the broadest sense, then, the ideas commonly associated with UFOs can be analyzed from the vantage point of Scripture.

The intent of this section is to briefly highlight a number of passages that have application, at least potentially, to some portions of the UFO movement. While in no way condemning the honest, scientific labors of many ufologists, there is a side to this phenomenon which simply must be addressed by the Christian community. To that end, what follows are some basic biblical criteria for interpreting and responding to segments of the UFO craze.

John 20:30-31
...30 Therefore many other signs Jesus also performed in the presence of the disciples, which are not written in this book; 31 but these have been written so that you may believe that Jesus is the Christ, the Son of God; and that believing you may have life in His name.

As John concludes his Gospel, he writes concerning the purpose of his writing. His goal is to show forth the identity of Jesus, and so lead people to embrace Him (v. 30). This He accomplishes by recording for us "signs" which Jesus performed.

A sign (Greek "semeion") is a token or indicator of something. For John, the "signs" he has in mind are the miracles which Jesus performed throughout His ministry. We know Jesus is who He claimed to be because, among other things, He performed supernatural wonders or signs. Jesus thus signaled by His amazing deeds that He truly is God's Messiah and unique Son, and thus worthy of all honor and trust.

This concept is important for our discussion of UFOs, for some have claimed that Jesus' miracles were merely technological and not supernatural. But this is contrary to the biblical record and the claims of Jesus. There is no indication that Jesus' miracles are intended merely to impress. The purpose of these marvelous deeds is to lead the reader to acknowledge the uniqueness of His person and role. In other words, Jesus doesn't imply some vague sort of superiority. He claims, rather, to be the divine Messiah.

This, once again, leaves us in a dilemma of sorts. Since Jesus is neither a misguided individual, nor a deceiver, we can't properly see Him as a kindly space-creature or some such thing. His signs must be accepted along with all that He spoke and did. Much more than technological marvels, Jesus' miracles demonstrate the truthfulness of His claims to messiah-ship and deity.

1 Corinthians 2:1-2

…1 And when I came to you, brethren, I did not come with superiority of speech or of wisdom, proclaiming to you the testimony of God. 2 For I determined to know nothing among you except Jesus Christ, and Him crucified.

Here we learn there are priorities to Christian life and ministry. And at the heart of what believers must maintain is "Christ crucified." The apostle says, in fact, that he desires to know nothing else! He doesn't mean, of course, that no other subject is worth considering. What does matter, though, is that Christ is the goal and centerpiece of Christianity. All truth is either a pointer to Christ, or a means of highlighting His many virtues.

When it comes to apologetics, therefore, we must strive to have a Christ centric, gospel-oriented focus. Christ is Lord. The Son is our hope. Jesus is the only worthy object of worship. As we explore the meaning of UFOs and aliens, let us not stray from the One who is the motive and goal of all truly Christian pursuits, the Lord Jesus Himself.

Galatians 1:6-12

…6 I am amazed that you are so quickly deserting Him who called you by the grace of Christ, for a different gospel; 7 which

is really not another; only there are some who are disturbing you and want to distort the gospel of Christ. 8 But even if we, or an angel from heaven, should preach to a gospel contrary to what we have preached to you, he is to be accursed! 9 As we have said before, so I say again now, if any man is preaching to you a gospel contrary to what you received, he is to be accursed! 10 For am I now seeking the favor of men, or of God? Or am I striving to please men?… 11 for I would have you know, brethren, that the gospel which was preached by me is not according to man. 12 For I neither received it from man, nor was I taught it, but I received it through a revelation of Jesus Christ.

Paul was an apostle, having been directly commissioned by the risen Jesus. Yet even he had to acknowledge the higher priority and authority of the divinely authorized message. In fact the exclusivity of the gospel demanded that all competing ideas be rejected. So it is here. Christian truth must be upheld at all costs; half-true pretenders must be discarded.

The instruction Paul gives may seem somewhat harsh to modern ears. To curse someone, after all, sounds a bit harsh. Yet the ramifications of the Christian gospel must not be ignored. If Christ really is God's Son and if He alone can supply redemption for fallen men, then all spurious gospels must be viewed as harmful.

"If, then, anyone proclaims something different, he comes under the judicial wrath of God![37]" As Paul says, "let him be accursed."

All of this is very pertinent to the discussion of UFO claims. If the UFO occupants, or believers in them, promote that which contradicts God's Word, they must be dealt with sternly. However we explain the phenomenon at least one thing is clear: Unbiblical messages mustn't go unchallenged (Jude 3-4).

2 Thessalonians 2:1-12

…1 Now we request you, brethren, with regard to the coming of our Lord Jesus Christ and our gathering together to Him, 2 that you not be quickly shaken from your composure or be disturbed either by a spirit or a message or a letter as if from us, to the effect that the day of the Lord has come. 3 Let no one in any way deceive you, for it will not come unless the apostasy come first, and the man of lawlessness is revealed, the son of destruction, 4 who opposes and exalts himself above every so-called god or object of worship, so that he takes his seat in the temple of God, displaying himself as being God… 7 For the mystery of lawlessness are already at work; only he who now restrains will do so until he is taken out of the way. 8 Then that

---

[37]Richard N. Longenecker, Galatians (WBC; Dallas, TX: Word Books, 1990), p. 18.

lawless one will be revealed whom the Lord will slay with the breath of His mouth and bring to an end by the appearance of His coming; 9 that is, the one whose coming is in accord with the activity of Satan, with all power and signs and false wonders, 10 and with all the deception of wickedness for those who perish, because they did not receive the love of the truth so as to be saved. 11 For this reason God will send upon them a deluding influence so that they will believe what is false, 12 in order that they all may be judged who did not believe the truth, but took pleasure in wickedness.

In context, Paul is dealing with events that are precursors to "the Day of the Lord[38]." That "day," Paul writes, cannot arrive until a number of historical incidents take place. Among these are an end time apostasy and the revealing of the man of lawlessness. While neither has occurred yet, "the mystery of lawlessness is already at work" (v. 7); that is, a Satanic scheme is already in place. At the same time, Paul surely wants his readers to be aware of these eschatological realities. The world, even now under the sway of dark forces, will one day experience the full unleashing of Antichrist's power.

---

[38] The Day of the Lord includes judgment and deliverance, wrath and joy. At that time God will be vindicated, Christ glorified, His enemies put down, and believers blessed. See Ernest Best, A Commentary on the First and Second Epistles to the Thessalonians (1972; Peabody, Mass: Hendrickson Publishers, 1986), p. 206.

Concerning the subject of UFOs, it is surely helpful to consider these strange happenings in light of this description of the man of lawlessness. Notice his amazing deceptiveness[39]. He is able to cause people to believe a lie, leading them to ultimate judgment. And he can perform, by the hand of Satan himself, powerful signs and false wonders[40]. Of course, no one can be sure what these wonders entail. Neither are we in a position where we can place all UFOs with certainty in the category of Antichrist. What can be said, though, is that certain incredible miracles will occur at the end of the age. These will be so alluring that many will be misled.

Much of what surrounds the UFO phenomenon

---

[39] During His Olivet Discourse, Jesus speaks of the deception of the last days (Mark 13:21-23). He tells us, among other things, that the "signs and wonders" of false teachers are designed to lead people astray. In fact, false Christ's intend to deceive, "if possible, the elect" (v. 22). Whatever else this involves, the impression given is of a deception so alluring that only the elective purpose of God can preserve His children. In light of the claims made by some within the UFO fold, Jesus' words are both frightening and comforting. The terror results from considering the amazing abilities of false prophets. Thankfully, the joy comes in knowing that God is far greater than His enemies, and He's on our side!

[40] "All three of these words (i.e., power, signs, and wonders) are used of the miracles of Christ. They are probably used for that reason. They help us to see the counterfeit nature of the Man of Lawlessness. The first term denotes the supernatural force which actuates the miracles. The second points to their character as directing attention to something beyond themselves. The third, 'wonders,' reminds us that miracles are things which man cannot explain. He can only marvel at them." Leon Morris, The First and Second Epistles to the Thessalonians (1959; reprint, NICNT; Grand Rapids: William B. Eerdmans Publishing Co., 1989), p. 231.

is condemned by Scripture. Furthermore, some of the events connected to these unbiblical segments of ufology are at least amazing, if not miraculous. While proving nothing outright, these parallels serve to warn believers that they should approach this phenomenon with discernment. Thankfully, the wisdom required is amply supplied in the apostolic traditions, in which Christ's followers are exhorted to "stand firm" (2 Thessalonians 2:15).

1 John 4:1-4

...1 Beloved, do not believe every spirit, but test the spirits to see whether they are from God, because many false prophets have gone out into the world. 2 By this you know the spirit of God: every spirit that confesses that Jesus Christ has come in the flesh is from God; 3 and every spirit that does not confess Jesus is not from God; this is the spirit of the antichrist, of which you have heard that it is coming, and now it is already in the world. 4 You are from God, little children, and have overcome them; because greater is He who is in you than he who is in the world.

John tells us to "test the spirits" (v. 1). This implies at least the following:

1) False ideas permeate this world;
2) Personal spirit beings are responsible for doctrine;
3) These "spirits" are to be tested;
4) Some criteria exists by which we can

perform such testing;

5) Christians are responsible and equipped for identifying and opposing false ideas and embracing good ones.

In context John identifies and contrasts two opposing "spirits"; one of error, the other of truth (v. 6). The determining factor as to which category a given teaching belongs is this: "How do these spirits, as they promulgate their doctrine, relate to Jesus Christ?" The apostolic position is that Jesus came in the flesh. That is, the Son of God actually became a man for man. He was "revealed in the flesh" (1 Timothy 3:16). Anyone, John says, who doesn't confess this Jesus "is not from God" (v. 3). "Since it is the great work of the Holy Spirit to testify about Christ and exalt Him (John 16:13-14), the person of the Lord Jesus becomes the touchstone of truth or error [41]." Those who deny the realities surrounding Jesus align themselves with the spirit of Antichrist. Still, false prophets cannot ultimately destroy God's "overcoming" children, for "greater is He who is in [them] than he who is in the world" (1 John 4:4).

Though the spirit of Antichrist is already in the world (v. 3) one day it will manifest itself in fuller ways. Thus Christians must examine the ideas and teachings they

---

[41] David Jackman, The Message of John's Letters (BST; Downers Grove: IL, InterVarsity Press, 1988), p. 11.

encounter. Regarding the subject of UFOs, it is certainly right to make reasonable judgments [42] (John 7:24; 1 Thessalonians 5:21-22). No conscientious Christian should undervalue this responsibility. Indeed, no ufologist should fear the results of such testing. According to John, the discerning individual is one who "test's the spirits to see whether they are from God."

---

[42] "In an age when Matthew 7:1 ('Do not judge, or you too will be judged') has replaced John 3:16 as the only verse in the Bible the man in the street is likely to know, it is perhaps worth adding that Matthew 7:1 forbids judgmentalism, not moral discernment. By contrast, John 7:24 demands moral and theological discernment in the context of obedient faith (7:17), while excoriating self-righteous legalism and offering no sanction for censorious heresy hunting." D.A. Carson, The Gospel According to John (Grand Rapids: William B. Eerdmans Publishing Company, 1991), p. 317.

Chapter 10: A Theological Framework for the Space-Age

A right minded approach to UFOs involves the recognition and implementation of biblical parameters or principles. It's not, of course, that the Scriptures contain an exhaustive catalogue of every subject. Rather, the Bible provides a basic framework for interpreting life. To that end, here are some of the more helpful pieces of theological truth.

God as Speaker

God is a talking God. He communicates with His creatures. This He has done in various ways, with the pinnacle of divine revelation coming in His Son. (Hebrews 1:2). The ramifications of such a truth are, of course, staggering. There is purpose to our existence, for God can be known through Jesus Christ. And there is direction to life as well, since we possess, through Christ's appointed emissaries, the objective criteria of God's written Word.

What this means for our UFO studies is that we possess an interpretive grid; a means of determining reality, a standard of righteousness. While this doesn't clear up the UFO dilemma, it does provide us with some of the stability, wisdom, and direction we all desperately need.

Sadly, not all Christians immerse themselves in biblical truth. But those who prayerfully make a commitment to knowing the mind of God in Scripture operate at a distinct advantage in studying the UFO phenomenon. In the midst of much uncertainty, we possess the theological anchor of God's Word (Psalm 119:96; Mark 13:31).

God as Creator

Many of the messages which supposedly originate from outer space assume the validity of macro-evolution. In fact, it is reported that some of the "aliens" say their mission is to help us evolve to the next level.

All of this is a clear contradiction of the Bible's claim that God is Creator (Genesis 1:1). He is the One who spoke the universe into existence (Psalm 8:3; 89:11). All by Himself He fashioned the heavens and the earth[43].

This means that whatever UFOs are, they are the product of God's creative hand. Are they angels, fallen or unfilled? Then God formed

---

[43] For a sampling of literature which supports biblical creationism, see Phillip E. Johnson, *Darwin on Trial* (Downers Grove, IL: InterVarsity Press, 1993); *The Creation Hypothesis*, ed. J.P. Moreland (Downers Grove, IL: InterVarsity, 1994); Nancy R. Pearcey and Charles B. Thaxton, *The Soul of Science: Christian Faith and Natural Philosophy* (Wheaton, IL: Crossway Books, 1994).

them. Are they visitors from a different world or another dimension? If so, the Lord is responsible for their existence.

God as Ruler

The Bible is replete with statements of God's sovereignty. He is King, with no competitors (Isaiah 46:9-10). Thus all life, both good and evil, must be seen as an unfolding of His eternal plan. To put it another way, nothing happens by chance. Our reigning Lord is the ultimate controller of all that happens in this world; and all other worlds are under His care as well (Ephesians 1:11; Colossians 1:16).

Let's say, then, that UFOs are extraterrestrial or perhaps angelic or some other explanation. Whatever the case, their influence or appearance is no surprise to God. It's all part of His sovereign decree. If UFOs land on the White House lawn, the only proper conclusion will be that God planned it that way. Since He is sovereign, we needn't fret at any prospect. Almighty God reigns, and nothing escapes His grasp.

God as All Powerful

The writers of Scripture tell us that God is an awesome, transcendent Being. Never is He presented as a partially powerful deity. On the contrary, all power is at His disposal. Indeed, He is able to rule the universe because His strength knows no bounds.

Thus the idea that God is some ancient astronaut not only contradicts various passages of the Bible, but is also contrary to the God therein presented. Isaiah asks, "To whom then will you liken God? Or what likeness will you compare with Him?" (40:18). Clearly the Lord has no peer. "Our God is in the heavens; He does whatever He pleases" (Psalm 115:3). Or as the angel Gabriel stated to Mary, "Nothing is impossible with God" (Luke 1:37).

As mentioned previously, this means that no extraterrestrial or angel is a fit replacement for the mighty Yahweh. Neither is any created being a match for His incomprehensible power.

God as Savior

It is one thing to create, speak, and rule. It's quite another to love and care. This is especially true when the objects of that love are rebels who deserve nothing good (Romans 5:6-8). But this is the portrait of God we find in the Bible. The Lord is merciful and compassionate. In a word, He is a God of grace (John 3:16; 1 John 4:9-10).

But how does this affect the study of UFOs? Well, it helps in at least a couple of ways. For one, it is imperative to see the Savior as the centerpiece of biblical interpretation. Our primary search isn't for UFOs in the Bible, but for an increased knowledge of and appreciation for the Son of God. This, in turn, should be reflected in our lives. However much effort we expend in studying these strange ideas, we mustn't allow our priorities to get out of kilter. Only with Jesus Christ at the center of our lives are we able to face any reality, even that presented by UFOs.

God as Provider

Not only is it true that God has rescued us from sin, hell, and futility by the cross of the Savior. He has also provided the strength, inward motivation, and divine counsel needed for successfully maneuvering our way through life. This is provided chiefly by the Holy Spirit (John 14:16-18). The Spirit refreshes us and paves our way; He leads us into an apprehension of the Savior, and an understanding of truth.

Christian investigation, therefore, is not to be performed in a vacuum. Instead, we are to live in active dependence on the Spirit who instructs primarily through His Word (John 14:23-26; 16:13-15). Apologists must consciously ask for His leading as they seek biblically accurate and God-honoring answers to the mystery of UFOs.

Christianity

Christianity is about God and His revelation to mankind. The Lord of the universe has communicated with His creatures and this so they might know and serve Him. The Word of God (i.e., the Bible) speaks of God, and God speaks by means of His Word. For the believer this means that an acquaintance with Scripture leads to a knowledge of God. Likewise, dependence on God enables one to comprehend and inculcate the inscripturated message. As Carl Henry has stated:

"...The ontological axiom of Christian theology is the existence of the God of the Bible, and the epistemological axiom is divine revelation. All the truths of revealed religion flow consistently from these first principles. Human reason is not the creative source of truth but is a divinely fashioned instrument for recognizing truth, nor is a demand for verification of theological claims inappropriate to Christian theology. The Christian verification principle is not inner faith or sense experience or moral effect or cultural consensus. It is revealed Scripture. The inspired Bible is the proximate and universally accessible statement of the cognitive content of divine revelation[44]."

In other words, Christians are people with commitments, both to God and His Word. Likewise, they possess the framework necessary for evaluating the ideas which

---

[44]Carl F.H. Henry, *Gods of this age or God of the ages?* (Nashville, TN: Broadman & Holman Press Publishers, 1994), p. 250.

daily swirl around them. As prayerful believers saturate their minds with divine truth, they acquire a measure of the wisdom needed to be spokesmen for the gospel of Jesus Christ. This wisdom serves as a spiritual/moral compass, properly directing them through this sometimes baffling world.

As Christian apologists it is our privilege to defend, explain, and clarify the truth in the context of contemporary culture. This includes grappling with puzzling subjects like UFOs. Of course, complete answers to the many questions spawned by this phenomenon are elusive. Still, the Christian does have a starting point. With God as King, His Word the rule, Jesus as Savior and the Spirit the divine enabler, believers possess the stability and foundation necessary for comprehending and coping with reality.

To that end, here are some principles for constructing a UFO apologia:

1) The Bible is the only sure foundation for thought and life. Scripture is the measuring stick of all truth claims. Whatever the precise identity of UFOs, they must be viewed and dealt with from a biblical stance. In order to be effective thinkers (Psalm 119:66, 98-100, 130) and apologists (Philippians 1:7, 16, 27; 1 Peter 3:15) Christians must prayerfully immerse their minds in

biblical truth, and "contend earnestly for the faith which was once for all handed down to the saints" (Jude 3). Blessings come to those who are "humble and contrite of spirit, and who tremble at [God's] word" (Isaiah 66:2).

2) <u>Christ is the centerpiece of Christian apologetics.</u> Christians mustn't leave their first love (Revelation 2:1-7). It is imperative to see all apologetic endeavors as a means to a greater end, i.e., knowing and experiencing the Savior. Only when preoccupied with Him is there protection from error and wrong priorities. He must remain the joy and stabilizing influence of our lives. UFOs, as fascinating and relevant as they may be, are not intended to be an idol. Jesus alone is the object of worship and place of safety.

3) <u>All believers should strive to be innovative spokesmen for the truth.</u> Too often believers are stagnant and ineffective when it comes to proclaiming the gospel. One reason is a lack of concern to communicate in fresh and challenging ways. Another is the inability to discern the issues which dominate the modern world. In order to be successful messengers of the good news, it is necessary to grapple with those themes which dominate contemporary society. Today this includes a right-minded appraisal of the UFO

phenomenon. Such an endeavor must be approached prayerfully, biblically, and with open eyes. Let us, therefore, remain faithful to the task before us, undaunted by any alien agenda, and never wavering in our allegiance to Jesus the Lord. With Paul, may our mission be "the defense and confirmation of the gospel" (Philippians 1:7, 16, 27).

Chapter 11: A Christian Response to a Modern Trend[45]

In recent history the comet Hale-Bopp was seen streaking across the earth's skies, and many looked to capture a glimpse of this rather rare celestial event. But members of the Heaven's Gate cult had visions of a different sort; they thought a massive UFO might be riding in the wake of the comet, and that this UFO could transport them to a better world. The cult's leader, named Do (as in dough)[46], considered himself to be a Christ-like figure, and led his New Age followers to believe that mass-suicide ("leaving these containers," as they put it) was the means of escape to "the level above." Since this occurrence, the subject of religious cults and their bizarre belief systems has been much discussed. Once again, UFOs are in the news.

For many people of common-sense the whole scene appears ludicrous. Surely, the beliefs of groups such as Heaven's Gate pose no threat for the sane individual. Or do they? Is there something relevant to glean from this tragedy? Are there lessons we

---

[45]The writing of this chapter was motivated by the events surrounding the March 1997 mass-suicide of thirty nine members of the Heaven's Gate cult near San Diego. Our commentary, however, extends beyond the extreme activities of this single group to the extremely influential UFO/New Age phenomenon.

[46]Marshall Applewhite, the cults co-founder and leader, was known by various names including "Father John," "Bo," and the above mentioned "Do." He apparently had an interest in reincarnation and UFOs, and held to a gnostic-like religious philosophy.

should learn and take to heart? Thirty-nine deluded individuals left this earth to stand before their Maker. Their legacy is, at the heart, religious in nature. Therefore, true believers in Jesus Christ should have something to say about these matters.

1) <u>False teachers will always be among us.</u> Jesus warned that there would be false teachers among us who would mislead many (Matthew 7:15; 24:11), and His words have been fulfilled countless times throughout history. In the early days of the Church some denied Christ's humanity, while others denied His deity. A large segment of the professing church even erred when it came to understanding how men can know God. Other errors (e.g., invalid Greek arguments for the primacy of human reason) have been more subtle. But false teaching is not merely an ancient problem; it is one which still haunts us today. Included here are various cults and false religions, atheistic secularism (which denies the need for God), and evolutionary theory. The faces and methods may change, but the message always leads in the same direction, away from Christ and the teachings of the Bible. The Heaven's Gate scene in San Diego is but one, very sensational, example of what occurs daily throughout our land. Buying into religious deception is a way of life for many people. And this reminds us that

evil forces really do exist. As Paul stated centuries ago, "our struggle is…against the spiritual forces of wickedness in the heavenly places" (Eph 6:12).

2) <u>Even intelligent people are susceptible to deception.</u> In our pseudo-intellectual age, the prevalent notion is that "education"; scientific and secular know-how; is all we need to shield us from foolish choices. Of course, there is some truth to this idea, proper education can dispel ignorance. But secular man is usually unaware of other factors which play a role in the decision making process. Man's heart is deceptive and easily led astray (Jeremiah 17:9; Mark 7:20-23). And, as mentioned above, there are spiritual forces which leave their mark on humanity. Indeed, the prince of these forces is said to lead people captive at his will (2 Tim 2:26)! Although a number of those involved in the situation in San Diego were characterized as intelligent, this evidently was no buttress against the moral and spiritual deception they experienced. Something greater than personal ability is required for fortification against error, we need the Spirit of Truth; the third member of the triune Godhead. He, Jesus said, leads us to a knowledge of God (John 15:26). Likewise, the Spirit has given us the Word of Christ (Col 3:16), by which we can

discern the difference between truth and error (I John 2:20). Wisdom dictates, therefore, that Christians avail themselves to those influences which draw them toward their Lord, and thereby protect themselves from spiritual chicanery. The bottom-line here is that anyone, even believers, can be led astray. We must determine in advance, then, to "be strong in the Lord, and in the strength of His might" (Eph 6:10).

3) The popular UFO movement can be dangerous. Few contemporary concepts have had a more powerful, though sometimes inconspicuous, impact on modern man than the UFO phenomenon[47]. From motion picture movies and TV programs to popular literature on the subject, UFOs are a part of the American psyche. While most people never take the UFO mentality to the extreme witnessed in the Heaven's Gate cult, many have gradually succumbed to popular New Age concepts. Polls have shown that a large percentage of Americans believe in life on other worlds. Often the belief in extraterrestrial creatures has taken on a religious flavor. In fact, an increasing number of individuals believe

---

[47] One analysis of a Gallup poll suggests that for every Christian there are five UFO enthusiasts, and that these UFO believers outnumber the voters who placed our last three Presidents in office. See Phil Cousineau, *UFOs: A Manual for the Millennium* (New York: Harper Collins Publishers, 1995), p. 179.

there is some tie between space visitors and ancient religion. This was popularized some years ago by Erich Von Daniken, and today millions have been influenced in similar ways through the writings of men like Zecharia Sitchen[48]. Even among those who aren't exposed to official "alien" propaganda, there is a tendency in our day to explain all of life via higher technology. When speculation goes unchecked, you are left with a technological model of life in which much of our religious history is explained in terms of extraterrestrial visitors. Though many Christians are prone to dismiss the UFO movement as mere fanaticism, there is an undeniable societal trend toward "alien" religion. That is many are willing to place alleged extraterrestrials in the category of creator-savior[49]. Surely, this is an unbiblical philosophy, and one which is a cause for concern among Christian people. The Church must be prepared to

---

[48]Erich von Daniken is the Swiss writer whose book *Chariot of the Gods?* sold more than 25 million copies in the 1970s. Sitchen's books, which are of a more scholarly tone, include *The Twelfth Planet* and *Stairway to Heaven* which became part of a series known as the *Earth Chronicles*. Recently, he has published his interpretation of the book of Genesis, which he titles *Genesis Revisited*. These men and many others have helped to popularize the idea that ancient astronauts (aliens) play a major role in earth's history.

[49]The Bible does not appear to speak to the issue of possible life on other worlds. What we do know is that earth is the object of God's special attention, the theological/redemptive center of the universe. Whether or not the current New Age messages originate in outer space is irrelevant on this point. Any teaching which contradicts/denies the Word of God must be deemed invalid, deceptive, and anti-Christian

give answers within our contemporary milieu, even when this involves dealing with those whose claims are "out of this world."

As Christian apologists we should be cognizant of the matters we have addressed here:
- ➤ False teaching will always be with us;
- ➤ All of us are susceptible at some level to deception;
- ➤ The UFO phenomenon is one current route by which error is promulgated.

It is essential that we "contend earnestly for the faith" (Jude 3) within our contemporary culture. This involves being well grounded in biblical truth;
- ➤ What is the gospel?
- ➤ What does it offer modern man?
- ➤ How does the Christian answer modern dilemmas?

Furthermore, we must counter current arguments of an anti-Christian nature, including those propagated by believers in alien religion and UFO encounters. The fringe elements of this movement, the type popularized in the tabloids, must not be allowed to blind us to the reality that many individuals have, consciously or otherwise, bought into a quasi-religious brand of UFOlogy[50]. May God enable us to

---

[50] Although most of the Church has ignored the UFO phenomenon, there is some good literature on the subject. Clifford Wilson

center our lives in the true "man from heaven," Jesus Christ (1 Cur 15:47). He alone provides the stability needed for the task of evangelizing the misguided people of our modern world.

has written *Crash Go The Chariots*, *The Chariots Still Crash* (both refutations of Erich von Daniken's ideas), and *The Alien Agenda*. More recently, there is William Alnor's *UFO's in the New Age* (Grand Rapids: Baker Book House, 1992). Also of interest are the works of Jacques Vallee, one of the premier investigators in the field of UFOlogy. Though Vallee is no friend to Christianity, his interpretations of the UFO phenomenon sound remarkably biblical. See especially his *Revelations: Alien Contact and Human Deception* (New York: Ballantine Books, 1991).

Chapter 12: UFOs - Does Anybody Care? The Need for a Cutting-Edge Apologetic

How is it, with all the proliferation of UFO material, that the Christian Church would remain so silent, so uninformed about what is certainly one of the most influential movements of our day.

There are, of course, a number of reasons for the Church's absence from these affairs. For some, the claim that extraterrestrials are among us seems too extreme and far-fetched to be taken seriously.

For others, their ignorance stems from the simple lack of contact with the people and happenings of the real world. But whatever the cause, most Christians have done little to stem the tide created by belief in what might be termed the alien agenda.

It is high time, therefore, to provide a biblical framework for understanding and interpreting the UFO phenomenon. This chapter is written to that end, to show the validity of UFO research by believers, and to provide principles for interpreting this modern mystery.

Why study UFO's?

➤ <u>It is the duty of the Church to confront, and offer alternatives to, the prevailing trends of the age and one particularly dominant motif is the UFO phenomenon.</u>

o Since its inception, the Church has had to cope with the numerous spiritual counterfeits that threaten its existence. From faulty views of the person of Jesus Christ to heretical teachings on salvation. Error has always required analysis, denunciation, and the implementation of biblical alternatives. But none of this can occur unless Christians become watchers of contemporary culture.

For example, when Paul went to Athens he looked at the surroundings and sought to make sense of what he had observed (Acts 17:16). As a result, his presentation of the good news was contexualized. That is, he was able to base it on what he knew of the Athenian culture to communicate the truth in ways relevant to the Athenian people. Therefore, one major factor in Paul's efforts to evangelize was his cognizance of culture.

It is important for us as well to know something of the cultural milieu in which we find ourselves. Among the ideas permeating society is the UFO phenomenon. Anyone paying attention to the times would have a difficult time ignoring the great UFO influence. This being the case, it is only right for Christian apologists to look into and offer suggestions for interpreting this phenomenon. In other words, it is indeed reasonable and proper for believers to construct a UFO apologetic[51].

➢ The rampant pluralism of our day has created an environment in which almost anything, including UFOs, is given credence.

o We live in a time when nearly everything is deemed acceptable, and nothing absolutely certain. Live and let live is an apt description for many people today. This explains, in part, the emergence of so many new religious beliefs. It is becoming increasingly common to find an array of world views, from Hinduism to New Age thought. Such diversity has made it easier to believe just about anything. If you want to worship an idol, not many will stand in your way. Would you prefer to channel a higher power? Few will

---

[51] By UFO apologetic I mean the effort to provide a framework for analyzing, deciphering, and responding to the ideas often associated with this phenomenon.

object.

Freedom, of course, is a noble concept. But freedom apart from parameters can only lead to anarchy and the toleration of nearly any world view. Predictably, then, as the Western world succumbs to this twisted version of liberty, many things which society used to frown upon receive approval.

It is no surprise then, that all kinds of fringe ideas have become mainstream. One such example is the UFO phenomenon. Though there is a huge UFO sub-culture, it is impossible to miss the more obvious influence of aliens on our society. If just about anything is allowable and if men and women are encouraged to give expression to their beliefs, it is inevitable for movements once considered ludicrous to flourish. Such is the fruit of religious and philosophical pluralism[52].

➤ There is a growing and influential UFO subculture.

---

[52] One characteristic of paganism is that is provides no absolute barometer for judging right from wrong. Thus it produces people who like the Athenians of old; "[spend] their time in nothing other than telling or hearing something new" (Acts 17:21).

o Besides the fact that aliens have become a popular theme, another less-known factor also threatens the Christian Church. This threat comes via the information highway, i.e., the Internet. As a quick investigation on any of the search engines reveals, UFOs and UFO religion are major topics. The sheer number of web sites should cause us to take notice, while the contents of some of them ought to breed a greater amount of seriousness among the Christian community.

As many believers go their own merry way, paying little attention to ufology, an often insidious UFO subculture promotes its agenda. Ironically, the lack of interest among Christians, coupled with the anonymous nature of Internet communication, may actually serve to fuel interest in UFOs.

On the one hand, there are those who make light of the possibility of any serious UFO discussion. On the other hand, many who do investigate this subject come away convinced that something really is going on. Where then is a person convinced of the reality of the phenomenon, yet too embarrassed to speak about it, to turn? That's easy: The Internet. Cyberspace provides a perfect environment for soaking in the phenomenon, without having to publicly admit it. Christians, therefore, need to become aware of this powerful underground movement.

➢ Ideas are important, and some of the ideas promoted by UFO adherents are extremely deceptive and dangerous.

o Heresy breeds more heresy, as one idea spawns another and then another and so on. With UFOs this is especially true. Though there are a number of investigators whose interest is primarily scientific, countless individuals have been attracted to the religious dimension of this phenomenon. Indeed, many are looking for salvation from the sky, and it isn't Christian doctrine they are seeking.

One extremely enticing thought for some, with a number of different twists, is the belief that extraterrestrials, not God almighty, created man. Some writers even go so far as to attribute the life and miracles of Jesus to alien technology. Countless people are open to the possibility of a technological deity, a replacement god who comes in the form of extraterrestrial intelligence.

As strange as this might sound to some readers, it is nonetheless an increasingly popular notion [53] . Therefore, because certain strands of ufology are unquestionably dangerous, Christian apologetics surely has a legitimate role to play in deciphering the truth claims of "alien" visitors.

An Approach to the Phenomenon

If the depiction given above is even remotely accurate, we are witnesses to a major new religious perspective, one which can be as deceptive as it is elusive. In light of these facts, it is incumbent upon believers to probe these matters further.

Whatever the truth about extraterrestrials, the UFO phenomenon has so permeated society that Christians must rise to the occasion and seek answers to this perplexing mystery. Though much more could be said, what follows are some broad categories to guide us in this quest.

➤ Be Biblical

o One mistake many investigators make is to attempt an analysis of the creation apart from the parameters and principles laid down by the Creator.

---

[53]Writers such as Zecharia Sitchen have gone a long way to showing the seeming plausibility of this idea. Sitchen's works include a series entitled *The Earth Chronicles* (six books in all), and *Genesis Revisited* (New York: Avon Books, 1990).

But God never intended for us to think, act, or analyze autonomously. Instead, He has provided an inspired paradigm, the Bible, through which we can make sense of reality. As to the subject of UFOs, it is of course true that the Bible is not some sort of UFO manual; but this doesn't render the Scriptures irrelevant when it comes to studying this phenomenon. Quite the contrary, the basic theme of alien religion is so often intertwined with the UFO agenda that it would be foolish to move forward without God's Word. The Bible, then, provides a framework for determining the possible identification of the ufonauts, as well as the basis for evaluating the validity of their claims.

➢ Be Balanced

o Balance is a rare commodity. When it comes to UFOs, for instance, many are prone to go to extremes. Some become full-fledged UFO fanatics, believers in alien redemption. Others deny the possibility of such stupendous claims, even though there is much research to warrant a serious appraisal of these matters. Believers, unfortunately, are not immune when it comes to excess.But Christians, of all people, should know the difference between a possibility (something that could happen) and a certainty (something that will happen). As we seek to place the UFO phenomenon beneath the lens of God's Word, let us remember to distinguish between theory and divine revelation. God's Word is certain and sure, but our understanding of the Bible and, especially of UFOs, is less than perfect. This means that more diligent efforts must be made, both to understand this phenomenon and to properly assess its significance biblically.

➢ Be gospel oriented

o At the end of the day, our chief purpose in doing apologetics is to lead people away from error and into the truth. In other words, our aim is to see those who are wrapped up in the UFO movement converted to the Savior. Let us strive, therefore, to keep the good news of Jesus Christ ever before the people we encounter. After all, it important not only to expose the dangers associated with this phenomenon, but also to highlight the beauty and attractiveness of God's glorious Son, heaven's true messenger.

Some Proposals and Thought-Provokers

A great variety of people study UFOs. Some

are out-and-out skeptics. Others are full-fledged believers. Many are somewhere in-between. Of course, a person's presupposition greatly influences what he allows himself to believe. Therefore, it is no surprise that a number of theories have been proposed as to the identity of UFOs. Among these are the following:

1) Hoaxes - A number of these have occurred. Some seek media attention and the thrill of fooling others. In fact, recent history had a couple of gentleman confessing to being the originators of a number of crop circles throughout England. There have even been reports of more elaborate hoaxes.

2) Overly active imagination - In our science-fiction crazed age, it is common for people to desire that which is unusual and out-of-the-ordinary. X-Files character Fox Mulder even has a poster in his office that exemplifies this trend. It reads: "I want to believe." Unquestionably, many do.

3) Misidentification of natural phenomenon - Most natural activity is known to the human observer. On occasion, however, there are happenings in nature that are out of the ordinary. Examples include the famous aurora borealis, certain types of cloud formations, and debris from outer space. These can be categorized as uncommon, yet natural phenomena. On top

of this, there are surely other natural wonders which science has yet to discover or categorize.

4) Misidentification of unknown technology - Made in the image of God, man possesses an inbred desire to create. Many of the technological wonders of recent years bear this out. From super-fast computers to stealth bombers, mankind has produced countless wonders. Since this is so, and because of the need for national security, it would be shocking if government groups haven't produced secret, "alien-like," technology. This doesn't necessitate an extraterrestrial source. A simpler explanation of human genius may be more viable.

5) Extraterrestrial visitors - This is the most popular view among ufologists. Aliens are, and have been, visiting our planet. The government has recovered alien craft. Aliens are among us. In fact, many believe that much of our technology was borrowed from extraterrestrial intelligences.

6) Terrestrial visitors - This is the less-popular theory that UFOs are of terrestrial origin. Perhaps they originate in the center of the earth. Maybe they live in some of the more remote places on earth (e.g., the poles, within volcanoes, etc.).

7) Inter-dimensional visitors - Because of the seemingly insurmountable distances an alien would have to traverse in order to arrive on planet earth, some have postulated aliens of an inter-dimensional sort. Rather that origination "way out there," they live along side us. These inter-dimensional beings are able to cross over into our dimension through sophisticated technology.

8) Angelic manifestations - This view resembles the inter-dimensional view. Depending on the author, this view relies more on a spiritual mechanism than a technological one for leaping between dimensions. Likewise, this view is often grounded in a Judeo-Christian world view. Therefore, the beings that jump from one dimension to another are angelic in nature.

These are merely a handful of the more popular theories on the reason for UFO sightings and other phenomena. The question remains though, which ones are most viable. While our purpose in this book is primarily to provoke thought, we can lay out some simple evaluative words.

Brief Analysis

All of the above theories have the potential of being true. Certainly, numbers (1) through (4) are part of the explanation for UFO sightings.

Number (5), on the other hand, is a reasonable possibility. From a Christian perspective, it is not impossible that God has created life elsewhere in the universe. On the other hand, current scientific knowledge does militate against alien civilizations being able to ever reach us in the first place. Some speculate that alien technology so transcends our own that it's no wonder we can't fathom it. At the end of the day, though, physical evidence is still quite scanty so far as proving the extraterrestrial hypothesis.

Number (6) the terrestrial aliens view is, I suppose, feasible. Most, however, don't go this route. Indeed, it does sound like a somewhat strange proposal. Then again, perhaps it's no more unlikely (weird?) than the extraterrestrial view.

Finally, we come to views (7) and (8). These, it seems to me, have a great measure of support in their favor. If inter-dimensional beings really do exist, this would explain their presence among us, without having to deal with the massive distances that extraterrestrials would need to travel. On top of this, scientists have already shown that other dimensions probably do exist. Of course, this work is all mathematical and theoretical. Still, not a few concede the existence of multiple dimensions. This doesn't prove that UFOs are inter-dimensional, but it certainly allows for the possibility.

Furthermore, the spiritual/religious aspects of this phenomenon seem to demand a spiritual explanation. This doesn't necessitate that we reject other viable alternatives. Neither does our explanation of these matters need to be simplistic and singular; in fact, a complex explanation of the phenomenon is probable. From a biblical perspective, however, it is difficult to ignore the reality that some portion, perhaps the majority, of this puzzling array of seemingly paranormal activity demands an inter-dimensional/angelic interpretation.

For Christians, the fundamental world view revealed in Scripture enables us to keep our feet on the ground, even as we find ourselves looking to the sky. More importantly, it causes us to ground our thoughts and hopes in the only One who truly warrants our praise, God's Son, Jesus Christ. May all our efforts to unfold life's mysteries be grounded in and guided by God's revealed truth. Therein is found stability, wisdom, and life.

www.ingramcontent.com/pod-product-compliance
Lightning Source LLC
Chambersburg PA
CBHW071825020426
42331CB00007B/1603